MYTHS ACROSS THE MAP

ZOMBIE MYTHS

Jenny Mason

Gareth Stevens
PUBLISHING

Please visit our website, **www.garethstevens.com**.
For a free color catalog of all our high-quality books,
call toll free 1-800-542-2595 or fax 1-877-542-2596.

CATALOGING-IN-PUBLICATION DATA

Names: Mason, Jenny.
Title: Zombie myths / Jenny Mason.
Description: New York : Gareth Stevens Publishing, 2018. | Series: Myths across the map |
Includes index.
Identifiers: LCCN ISBN 9781538214503 (pbk.) | ISBN 9781538213780 (library bound) |
ISBN 9781538214510 (6 pack)
Subjects: LCSH: Zombies--Juvenile literature.
Classification: LCC GR581.M37 2018 | DDC 398.21--dc23

Published in 2018 by
Gareth Stevens Publishing
111 East 14th Street, Suite 349
New York, NY 10003

Developed and Produced by Focus Strategic Communications, Inc.
Project Manager: Adrianna Edwards
Editor: Ron Edwards
Design and Composition: Ruth Dwight
Copy editors: Adrianna Edwards, Francine Geraci
Media Researchers: Adrianna Edwards, Paula Joiner, Maddi Nixon
Proofreader: Francine Geraci
Index: Ron Edwards, Maddi Nixon

PHOTO CREDITS: Credit Abbreviations: S Shutterstock; WC Wikimedia Commons. Cover, Title Page: Nomad_Soul/S; 4: Tithi Luadthong/S; 5: Igor Zh/S; 6, 7: Everett Historical/S; 8: karenfoleyphotography/S; 9: Captblack76/S; 10: neftali/S; 11 L: Daniel Cantero Pobes/S, R: Beth Swanson/S; 12: KPG_Payless/S; 13: jurasy/S; 14: Oleksandr Kavun/S; 15: drumdredd777/S; 16: Zvereva Iana/S; 17: Julymi/S; 18: Sergey Shubin/S; 19: L. Kragt Bakker/S; 20: Muslianshah Masrie/S; 21: Kiselev Andrey Valerevich/S; 22: Everett Historical/S; 23: Lyudmila2509/S; 24 L: patrimonio designs ltd/S, R: Vuk Kostic/S; 25: Dnalor 01/WC; 26: Kateryna Kon/S; 27: Anton_Ivanov/S; 28: Bin im Garten/WC; 29: Tithi Luadthong/S; 30: Pavel L Photo and Video/S; 31: Featureflash Photo Agency/S; 32: Kathy Hutchins/S; 33 L: Andrea Raffin/S, Background: leolintang/S; 34 TR: Chambers, Robert and Patrick, David. Chambers's Cyclopaedia of English Literature. London: W. & R. Chambers. 1901. 519. Internet Archive. Web. 16 May 2017, BL: Olga Popova/S; 35: Library of Congress/LC-USZ62-11916; 36: Featureflash Photo Agency/S; 37: Everett Historical/S; 38: Bin im Garten/CC 39: Jeff Cameron Collingwood/S; 40: Liew Weng Keong/S; 41 TR: torook/S, BL: Elliotte Rusty Harold/S; 42: Mikesilent/S; 43: Billion Photos/S; 44: Digital Storm/S; 45: vectorEps/S; Design Elements: Margarita Miller/S, viewgene/S, yoshi0511/S.

Printed in the United States of America

CPSIA compliance information: Batch CW18GS: For further information contact
Gareth Stevens, New York, New York at 1-800-542-2595.

TABLE OF CONTENTS

WHAT IS A ZOMBIE? 4

THE STAGGERING TRUTH 6

A GRAVE REALIZATION 13

KEEP CALM, CARRION 21

GOING VIRAL 29

A DEATH WISH 37

ZOMBIE MYTHS ACROSS THE MAP 45

GLOSSARY 46

FURTHER INFORMATION....... 47

INDEX 48

WHAT IS A ZOMBIE?

THE LIVING DEAD

A zombie is a reanimated corpse. Today, thanks to movies, video games, comic books, graphic novels, and television series, pretty much everyone has a good idea of what zombies are.

Zombies are usually thought to be mindless, slow, and unable to speak or think. They shuffle to get around. Whether moaning or growling, they are always on a relentless hunt for a mouthful of human flesh. As if that's not bad enough, they are infectious, meaning they can spread their condition to others.

Luckily, no matter how real they might appear on-screen, zombies are mythical creatures. Myths are popular beliefs rooted deep in the past. They are the stories we tell ourselves to explain the inexplicable or to cope with our deepest fears.

Zombies are easy to identify. Just look for the shuffle, listen for the moan, and sniff for the whiff of death.

DEAD AND GONE

Zombies have figured in humanity's stories for a very long time. All around the world, they symbolize something we have always feared—death. More specifically, people tend to fear what happens, and what cannot be explained, after death.

Zombies may also represent death on a grander scale: the **extinction** of humankind. Some cultures imagine the end comes with massive enemy invasions—a war so bloody that it forever extinguishes human life. The Norse legends of Iceland, Denmark, and Sweden, for example, refer to this final battle as the Ragnarök. In our modern culture, we envision extinction arriving with some lethal, incurable **pandemic** disease or perhaps some natural catastrophe beyond our control.

These days, in a strange twist of fate, zombies and their end-of-the-world antics may actually aid our long-term survival. Call it a unique case of the "living dead" helping the "dying live."

The Bible predicts the end of human civilization with the coming of Armageddon.

FAST FACT

According to the CIA's *World Factbook*, about two people die every second. Another way of looking at it: around 151,000 people die on your birthday. And very few of them will come back to life!

THE STAGGERING TRUTH

ENSLAVING THE SPIRIT

The word "zombie" has a couple of possible origins. *Nzambi*, the word for "god" or "deity," emerges from the Kongo language of west central Africa. Similarly, the Portuguese word *zumbi* implies a divine spirit or life force that exists in all people. That spirit could leave the body during dreams, or it could be possessed by another spirit. Lastly, special talismans, amulets, or charms could be steeped with the life force.

These words and ideas sailed halfway across the world inside slave ships. People from Africa were captured and shipped across the Atlantic to the Americas. There, they were forced to work the rest of their lives as unwilling slaves.

Slave ships, like the one in this 1790 diagram, packed people side by side like bottles.

FAST FACT

Between 1526 and 1867, some 12.5 million people were shipped from Africa in the Atlantic slave trade. Only 10.7 million arrived alive in the Americas.

AN INDOMITABLE SPIRIT

During the seventeenth and eighteenth centuries, many slaves wound up on what is now the Caribbean island of Haiti (then Saint-Dominique), where they labored on sugar plantations.

Conditions on the sugar plantations were brutal. Half of all the people sent to work there died within a couple of years.

Despite having left behind everything and everyone they knew, many slaves maintained their core spiritual beliefs. Most practiced and worshipped *voudon* or *voudou*, meaning simply "spirit." Voudon, or voodoo, dates back 10,000 years. Contrary to popular belief, it has little to do with sticking pins in dolls. In fact, it is a way of life intended to develop deep spiritual experiences.

Many slaves believed that when they died, their spirit would be freed and able to return home to Africa. Many slaves killed themselves rather than endure the savage conditions of enslavement. However, French Catholic plantation owners and operators tried to prevent suicides by convincing their slaves that the spirit of a suicide would spend eternity as a zombie skulking around the plantation.

THE DEVIL'S THRONE

Rumor has it that all the original 23 cemeteries of old New Orleans in Louisiana have a Devil's Chair hidden among the tombstones and crypts. The No. 1 St. Louis Cemetery houses the Devil's Throne. If you have the nerve, sit on that throne on a moonless night, and the devil will make you a zombie king or queen, able to cast spells and control people's souls.

Marie Laveau, a famous voodoo priestess, was said to have done just that in the 1800s. Allegedly, she was also gifted with everlasting life and beauty. She died in 1881 and is believed to be buried in No. 1 St. Louis Cemetery, the city's oldest burial ground.

Marie Laveau's grave is pictured here (above right). New Orleans has a high water table. Caskets that were buried underground sometimes floated to the surface. Therefore, above-ground tombs were much more common. This system also reflected the city's French and Spanish history.

HAUNTED SHADOWS

Meanwhile, in 1804, the voodoo religion gradually shifted its concept of zombies. Mythical tales arose claiming that sorcerers called *bokors* reanimated corpses. They brought bodies back from the dead and stripped them of their identity and free will by capturing their divine life force, or *zombie*.

The awakened undead allegedly had their tongues cut out. Deprived of speech and free will, these zombies were put to work in large labor camps or secret sugar plantations. In some sense, these legends illustrate how the Haitian people had thrown off their oppressors. But they had yet to shake off the lingering shadows and scars of a traumatic past.

Bokors were also known to capture the life force of a living person. They sealed this zombie essence inside bottles and sold them as good luck charms.

ZOMBIE HOMECOMING

In the 1980s, surprising evidence emerged that indicated the voodoo zombie myth might have some basis in fact. A man who had been dead and buried for 20 years suddenly reappeared and made contact with his family. He claimed to have been a zombie all that time, enslaved to a voodoo sorcerer.

Stories like this sprang up often in Haiti, but this one kicked off an international media storm. Not only could the man answer the most intimate and personal questions, but also his thumb matched the thumbprint pressed on the death certificate. Never had there been direct evidence to **corroborate** such wild tales!

ZORA THE ZOMBIE HUNTER

Award-winning African American novelist Zora Neale Hurston undertook zombie research in Haiti during the late 1930s. She interviewed many people who claimed that voodoo priests used animal toxins to poison and enslave their victims.

Zora Neale Hurston is pictured here in this US stamp from 2003.

A RECIPE FOR TROUBLE

The Haitian man claimed to have been poisoned. Although appearing dead, he had really been just paralyzed. Inside, he was awake and aware. He knew he was being buried alive but could not do anything to save himself. Finally, he was **exhumed** by a voodoo priest. He was brutally beaten and forced to take regular doses of drugs and poisons that rendered him senseless. For two decades, he labored as a zombie slave, until he finally escaped.

Harvard University ethnobiologist Wade Davis was called in to investigate. Davis discovered a core group of ingredients frequently used in the potions and spells of voodoo priests: toxins found in the ocean-dwelling bearded fireworm, the common tree frog, the giant toad, and the pufferfish.

bearded fireworm

pufferfish

Together, the ingredients extracted from these creatures form a dangerous potion that could cause paralysis and a sleep-like state. For example, a tiny amount of the **neurotoxin** in the pufferfish results in a coma-like state. Based on this evidence, Davis concluded that the stories about zombie slaves could be true!

STUBBORN MYSTERIES

Colleagues began to find problems with Davis's claims. For example, using the voodoo potion to put a body into a **catatonic** state is nearly impossible, as even the smallest doses of the voodoo potion are lethal. In addition, Haiti is a small island, yet no one has ever found the mass labor camps where zombies were supposedly sent to work. Nonetheless, Haitian media still continue to report cases of escaped zombies, while investigators try to uncover the truth behind the myths.

Before Haiti put a label on what is right now the world's most popular monster, reanimated zombie corpses walked the world under different names.

FUGU

Japanese diners pay a high price to dine on the nontoxic portions of meat inside the pufferfish, which they call *fugu*. Those who have ingested a direct dose of the neurotoxin and lived to tell about it report feeling locked inside their bodies, unable to move or communicate.

Fugu is a Japanese delicacy. The pufferfish is so poisonous that if the chef makes a mistake when slicing it, the result could be fatal to the diners. Its preparation is strictly controlled under Japanese law.

A GRAVE REALIZATION

DEAD WRONG

Besides looking hideous and smelling awful, dead bodies have always been viewed with a mixture of fear and mystery. The fear is that decaying corpses may spread disease among the living. The mystery arises because the process of decomposition presented ancient peoples with many seemingly unanswerable questions.

Why do the muscles of corpses sometimes spasm or jerk? Why do their joints lock with **rigor mortis**? Why do some cadavers, or corpses, take on purple or brownish zebra stripes (called liver mortis)? Modern medical science has only recently pinned these phenomena to complex but natural chemical processes inside the dead body. Meanwhile, other questions about death linger: Why do we grow old and die? Do bodies have a spirit, and if so, where does it go when the body decomposes?

FAST FACT

Corpse wax is a greasy, soap-like substance that oozes out of fatty cells as the body decomposes. Over time, the wax can harden into a shell, preserving the body inside.

A dead body undergoes countless changes.

MIDNIGHT STRIDES

Old tales from Germany tell of the *aufhocker*, a reanimated corpse with a habit of leaping out of its grave to ride piggyback on anyone out for a nighttime stroll. (The name means "leap upon" in German.) According to an ancient Hindu myth, the *vetala* is a ghostly spirit that uses cadavers like rental cars—animating them so it can get around.

Myths like these attempt to address the tricky questions of why dead muscles twitch or where spirits go after the body dies. Elsewhere in the world, the reanimated dead, or **revenants**, are seen as much more malevolent than pesky hitchhikers.

THE DRAUGR

The *draugr* of Norse folklore (plural: *draugar*) might be one of the most hostile and sinister zombies in the world. This revenant resides inside its grave, just like a similar monster called a *haugbui*. Unlike their *haugbui* cousins, *draugar* can leave their graves, by day or night, to hunt for their favorite food: human flesh and blood! They possess near superhuman strength and a few magical powers to boot. For instance, some *draugar* were able to cast curses, foretell the future, or shapeshift into cats.

Could a cat actually be a *draugr* in disguise?

SAGAS

The medieval Norse culture that was once prevalent in Scandinavian countries such as Sweden, Norway, and Denmark preserved the myth of the *draugr* in sagas. Sagas are long, epic story poems. They were shared orally over many generations and were eventually recorded in writing. In the *Eyrbyggja Saga*, the *draugr* Thorolf is described to be as big as an ox. And the *Grettis Saga* tells of Glámr, perhaps the most dreaded *draugr* of them all! *Draugar* were thought to form when a particularly strong will drew *hugr*, or the life force, back into a dead body.

According to Norse mythology, Valhalla is a beautiful place in the sky where warriors go after they die in battle.

FAST FACT

If a person had been exceptionally mean and greedy while alive, they were likely to come back from the dead and spend eternity as a *draugr*, a spirit in human form, instead of ascending to Valhalla.

SPIRITUAL CRISIS

For eons, the visible symptoms of bodily death defied reason and understanding, leading many to suppose that spirits or demons lived on in the corpse. Sometimes, a spirit sought revenge. Maybe it had failed to find its way into the afterlife. In some cases, a deity punished a spirit by transforming it into a demon condemned to roam the Earth in a rotting body rather than resting in peace.

ISHTAR'S ZOMBIE APOCALYPSE

In the *Epic of Gilgamesh*, one of the oldest surviving mythical texts from Mesopotamia (now Iraq and its neighboring countries), the goddess Ishtar threatens to raise the dead and send them after the living to eat their flesh. Basically, she plans to punish humankind with a zombie apocalypse.

In Mesopotamian mythology, Ishtar was an angel-like goddess of love, power, and war.

GLOBETROTTERS

Whatever the cause, being dead and rarely able to travel faster than a shuffle never stopped zombies from making their way into myths around the world. From the snowy Canadian wilderness to the temples of ancient China, from the icy Russian tundra to the Amazonian rainforests of Brazil, zombies get around.

GHOULISH GALS

Ancient Arab folklore warned travelers to beware of ghouls (*aghwal*; singular, *ghul*). These desert-dwelling shapeshifters might appear as animals, such as the hyena, or as beautiful women. In either form, they lured victims into the wastelands and devoured them.

In old Ukrainian tales, the *mavka* was another kind of undead seductress with long hair flowing down her back. Brush aside her hair and you'd see an open, fleshless back with its internal organs exposed. The *mavka* typically lured young men into forests and ate them.

CORPSE BRIDES

Once upon a time, a nervous bridegroom practiced reciting his wedding vows near a gravesite. A corpse in a wedding dress sprang from the moldering soil and claimed the man was now her husband. This particular tale is thought to have come from the sixteenth century in what is now northern Israel.

Fables involving corpse brides and ghost marriages exist across the map. Tim Burton based his 2005 animated movie *Corpse Bride* on the legend.

A RECIPE FOR TROUBLE

As illustrated by the zombie stories from Haiti, the only thing more frightening than a zombie is the zombie-maker—a living person, witch, or monster who can wake the dead. One example is the *isithfuntela* of West Africa. This witch was known for digging up dead bodies and resurrecting them for nefarious purposes.

In the 1870s, deep in the territory of the Arikara tribe — parts of Missouri, North Dakota, and Montana—medicine men **decapitated** warrior braves in front of white settlers and pioneers. These medicine men performed such rituals as a test of bravery, not a show of evil. They reattached the heads, and the warriors reportedly revived.

FAST FACT

Since zombies are not really alive, it is hard to "kill" them, but there are ways to slow and even stop them. Zombie hunters in movies and TV shows use explosives or flamethrowers to incinerate these monsters.

Chainsaws are a favorite weapon against zombies, but they may not be the most reliable. How would people fuel them with gasoline after the world comes to an end?

THE WENDIGO

Among the Algonquin tribes in North America, there was said to have existed a powerful monster—sometimes a spirit—known as the *wendigo*. Much like a voodoo priest, the *wendigo* was able to possess a body and enslave it. More often than not, the *wendigo* forced its slaves to commit unspeakable atrocities such as murder and cannibalism.

In 1879, a member of the Cree tribe staggered into a Catholic mission in St. Albert, in Alberta, Canada. His name was Swift Runner, and he claimed to be the lone survivor of a mysterious disease that overtook his household. An investigation of Swift Runner's story quickly revealed that he had murdered and eaten his mother, brother, wife, and six children! Swift Runner claimed to have been possessed by the *wendigo*. He was sentenced to death and hanged on December 20, 1879.

ZOMBIE DOGS IN THE SOUTHWEST

Zombie dogs were reportedly sighted near the Texas towns of San Antonio and Austin. The hairless, skinny mongrels were said to have enlarged fangs and a ravenous thirst for blood.

Investigators suspected some coyotes might have contracted a rare disease.

DROP-DEAD GORGEOUS

And yet, not all cultures exhibit a gloomy or frightful concept of death and the dead. In Mexico and Central America, *Día de Muertos* celebrations include large feasts, bright decorations, parades, dances, and depictions of the dead in whimsical costumes having a good time. Every October 31, families go to graveyards and celebrate at the gravesites of their dearly departed.

Similarly, the Torajan people of Indonesia honor the dead instead of fearing them in *ma'nene* rituals. Every three years in August, families travel to the countryside in order to clean up ancestral burial tombs. While there, they also enjoy a second funeral, or *ma'nene*. They dress the mummified bodies of the deceased in fine suits and bright colors. Coffins are lovingly tidied and the bodies respectfully returned to the ground.

At the *ma'nene* ritual in Indonesia, relatives clean off corpses and "walk" them back to their resting place.

KEEP CALM, CARRION

COMMON ZOMBIE TRAITS

Today, thanks to the feverish fandom of zombie movies, video games, and comic books, the modern myth of the zombie is truly global. The zombie's primary traits are widely recognized and unified.

For example, all zombies are newly dead (unlike mummies), brought back by radiation, chemicals, viruses, sorcery, or acts of deities. Also, they are very strong but neither fast nor agile. Their hunger, however, is relentless. Finally, they tend to be impervious to pain and injuries, except decapitation or a bullet to the brain.

APOCALYPSE NOW

Another common zombie trait is that they are often the cause of an end-of-the-world scenario, commonly called a "zombie apocalypse." An apocalypse is a chance to see into the future. We get to witness what the world might be like when the bonds of society break down, government and military forces collapse, and survivors huddle in small, isolated bands.

In contemporary science fiction, zombies are spawned from radioactivity, viruses, and misguided science experiments.

FAST FACT

Apocalypse does not mean "end of the world." It actually means "pulling back the veil."

THAT'S SICK

The unstoppable spread of zombies mirrors the terror associated with incurable pandemic diseases. For thousands of years, smallpox, measles, influenza, and cholera devastated human populations. Recent scares have included the deadly Ebola, West Nile, and Zika viruses. But these outbreaks are small compared to the Black Death (1347–1351) and the Spanish influenza (1918–1920).

OUTBREAKS

Moving like a battalion of evil spirits, the Black Death—bubonic plague—spanned borders, infecting millions on its journey across Asia and Europe. In just a few years, approximately one-third of the population in those areas perished. Bodies piled up in the streets. The stench of death was everywhere. Civilization fell apart, just as it does in the zombie apocalypse scenario popularized in films, books, and video games today.

Similarly, the Spanish influenza (now known as the H1N1 virus) affected 500 million people globally. In one year, the flu killed nearly as many people as the Black Death did in four. Unlike most diseases that target the elderly and small children, the virus mercilessly attacked the young and the healthy.

At Camp Dix, New Jersey, soldiers gargled with salt to prevent catching Spanish influenza.

FAST FACT

In the end, the bubonic plague is thought to have claimed between 75 and 100 million lives.

THE SIEGE

Zombies tend to swarm in vast hordes, surrounding small bands of survivors, similar to siege warfare. In a siege, an entire city or castle is barricaded against surrounding enemy forces, who use various tactics to penetrate the stronghold. If possible, the combatants cut off all access to incoming food and water, forcing the victims to either surrender or starve. Historically, sieges were common.

CITIES OF ASH

The Wall of Memory (shown here) in St. Petersburg, Russia, commemorates the people who perished during the siege.

The nomadic Visigoth tribes of Europe laid waste to Rome in the fifth century AD using siege tactics. After 1,000 years as the stronghold of a mighty empire, the "Eternal City" crumbled during the invasion of a zombie-like horde.

Similarly, the Mongols of East Asia besieged and destroyed the great cities bordering their grassy regions. In the mid-thirteenth century, they swarmed Baghdad, the jewel of the Middle East. The city, now the capital of Iraq, remained in ruins for hundreds of years.

Finally, in World War II, the Nazi army besieged the Russian city of Leningrad (now St. Petersburg). Survivors trapped inside the city endured horrors beyond any ever depicted in the goriest zombie movies. With no food to be found, some people even resorted to cannibalism! The Siege of Leningrad lasted almost two and a half years. It was one of longest and deadliest sieges in history, killing an estimated 1 million people.

PLEASED TO MEAT YOU

The zombie's hunger for flesh seems linked to the nearly universal taboo on cannibalism. Cannibals, like Swift Runner, are outcasts. They have long been unwelcome in the civilized world—a lesson demonstrated in many world myths.

The ancient Greeks told tales of Cronus, a Titan or divine being, who practiced cannibalism on his children. He ate the first five in order to guarantee that none would interrupt his reign. Zeus, the sixth child, not only survived but also defeated Cronus and imprisoned him for his crimes.

Cronus

Zeus

FAST FACT

In the 1990s, serial killer Jeffrey Dahmer was sentenced to life in prison for his crimes. Dahmer murdered 17 boys and men, eating many of them.

DEAD ENDS

Whether they are ancient or modern, all zombies are tough to defeat. Today's zombie manuals recommend a bullet or a long, sharp blade to lop off their heads. In the past, however, other tactics were used.

In the Middle Eastern country of Syria, archaeologists unearthed several mutilated bodies dating back to the Stone Age. Evidence suggested that sometime after their burial, the bodies were exhumed, and their heads were crushed and severed. Similarly in 2009, archaeologists in Ireland discovered two bodies, dating back to the eighth century, with rocks shoved into their mouths. In both cases, researchers speculate that these bodies must have been suspected of coming back to life and attacking the living.

SKULL AND CROSSBONES

The symbol of the skull and two crossed bones dates back to the fourteenth and fifteenth centuries. These were times of strife, war, and disease. The symbol was used as a reminder that death claims all lives eventually.

The chapel of bones in the Capuchin Crypt in Rome, Italy, houses entire rooms constructed from skeletal remains.

FEEDING FRENZY

A cadaver decays when bacteria in the digestive system and environment act like a cleaning crew. They gobble up the body tissues in a process called **autolysis**. That same cleaning crew can also spread infections. Bacteria are hardy single-celled microorganisms that survive just about anywhere—air, water, and your intestines. So human burial customs are, essentially, methods of bacterial waste disposal.

Bacteria are useful when turning milk into yogurt, but they are deadly when spreading infections such as pneumonia and food poisoning.

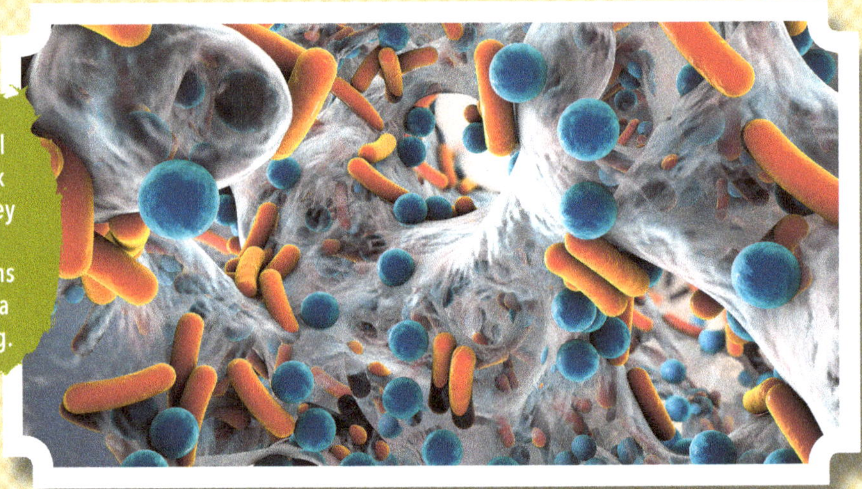

BURYING THE DEAD

Burial customs are also ways to honor the remains of a deceased loved one. For those who believe that the spirit remains inside the body for a while after death, a proper burial is essential. Otherwise, disturbing consequences might arise.

FAST FACT

The practice of burying the dead dates back over 100,000 years. Today, especially in large cities, the dead are often cremated and not buried.

ON PINS AND NEEDLES

For many cultures, piles of rocks or heavy tombstones conveniently marked graves—and kept the dead underground. But during the Middle Ages, unidentified diseases were linked to zombies, werewolves, and vampires. The only way to combat this evil was to dig up the suspect corpse, cut off its head, and drive a stake through the body. The stake pinned the body down, preventing the undead from further movement.

Norse lore suggested similar approaches to stopping a *draugr*'s resurrection. When preparing bodies for burial, Scandinavians bound the big toes or drove needles through the soles of the feet. Nobody likes to go around on pins and needles.

As far back as the second century BC, the *jiang shi* zombies or vampires climbed out of graves in China to devour the living as punishment for a poor burial. To prevent this, the Chinese wove ropes and tied intricate knots around dead bodies. They further tied the bound body into its coffin. If the body could not reanimate and wander about, then the spirit inside was more likely to find its way into the afterlife.

TERRACOTTA ARMY

During the late third century BC, the first emperor of China, Qin Shi Huangdi, had an army of 9,000 **terracotta** figures buried in his tomb. The warriors were meant to protect the emperor from *jiang shi* in his afterlife.

The Terracotta Army was uncovered in March 1974 by farmers digging a well in Xi'an, China. It is now a UNESCO World Heritage site.

CORPORAL PUNISHMENT

In ancient Greece, zombie prevention started before the burial with a practice called *maschalismos*, or mutilation of the body. Vital organs including the brain, heart, and liver were removed so that the buried body would be like a car with no engine.

Among the ancient peoples of what is today Germany and Eastern Europe, there lurked a zombie known as the *wiedergänger*, or "again-walker." To prevent the rise of one, Slavic burial customs prescribed a take-no-chances policy that involved binding the body, slitting the muscles and tendons, cutting off certain limbs, and driving a stake or cross through the heart. Lastly, a lump of dirt was jammed into the mouth.

DEATH-DEFYING ACTS

According to the Irish myth of Abhartach, zombies had to be buried vertically, as if doing a headstand. Abhartach was a dwarfish tyrant who repeatedly rose from the grave to heckle his enemies until finally, a rival chieftain buried him head first. The angry Abhartach never came back.

FAST FACT

According to some voodoo customs, the only way to stop a zombie is to feed it salt. A full teaspoon ought to kill a zombie in a minute or less.

This 700-year-old skeleton of a "vampire" was found in Bulgaria.

GOING VIRAL

DEAD BEATS

On Halloween, 2008, bloody, rancid, shuffling bodies staggered across the city of Nottingham, England. Moaning and groaning, they trudged to the Old Market Square, one of the busiest places in town, dense with people going about their daily business. These folks should have known what was coming. Rumors told of a similar invasion of the dead in Monroeville, Pennsylvania, the year before.

When the more than 1,200 zombies took over the square in Nottingham, the living stopped, stared, and waited. What was going to happen?

Abruptly, music blared through speakers and the zombies began to dance!

DEADLY DANCE

Starting in the early 2000s, "zombie walks" and zombie dances like those in England and Pennsylvania started off as small, fun events. People dressed up, put on convincing makeup, and gathered as a zombie horde. But as the zombie rose in popularity in movies and video games, zombie walks swelled.

By 2011, some cities around the world boasted zombie hordes 12,000 strong. In 2012, the annual zombie walk in Buenos Aires attracted 25,000 participants.

Many zombie walks function as excellent fundraisers for brain-related medical conditions, food banks, organ donor sign-ups, and blood donation drives.

Zombie walks take place around the world.

BURIED TREASURES

The ever-popular zombie hack 'em, slash 'em video game *Resident Evil* was released in 1996 and has since sold 75 million copies worldwide. Over time it has been revamped for new gaming systems and turned into six blockbuster films.

The world is currently enjoying a zombie tsunami. Zombies have also invaded comic books, graphic novels, and Japanese *manga* and *anime*. One such comic book series, *The Walking Dead* (2003), kicked off a megahit TV series by the same name. Since it began airing in 2010, the show has attracted nearly 20 million viewers around the world.

Based on the 2010 Isaac Marion novel, the film *Warm Bodies* is a Romeo-and-Juliet romance with zombies. The story asserts that a lifeless world is one without love. The cast are shown promoting the movie in 2013.

LETHAL DOSES

We want zombies the way we want marshmallows in our cereal! We dress up like them for Halloween. We feature them in movies such as the hit mash-up *Pride and Prejudice and Zombies*, which spices up elegant Georgian England with plenty of zombie guts and gore.

Zombies called "wights" also lurk in the *Dungeons and Dragons* role-playing game, not to mention the pages of J.R.R. Tolkien's *The Lord of the Rings* series, George R.R. Martin's *A Song of Ice and Fire* novels, and other popular books such as *Miss Peregrine's Home for Peculiar Children*. Even *draugar* make an appearance in *The World of Warcraft* as the race of Kvaldir.

But how did we get here? How did life get so saturated with zombies?

Douglas Booth, one of the stars of *Pride and Prejudice and Zombies*, appeared at the movie's premiere in Hollywood on January 21, 2016.

FAST FACT

Ransom Riggs is the author of *Miss Peregrine's Home for Peculiar Children*, a hit young adult novel published in 2011. It was Riggs's first novel. He followed with sequels in 2014 and 2015. Then, in 2016, Tim Burton directed the film version.

George Romero (left) is shown here in 2009. In his 1968 movie, nuclear radiation, not magic, wakes the dead across the Eastern seaboard. Since its premiere, *Night of the Living Dead* has grossed $30 million internationally.

ZOMBIES IN HOLLYWOOD

The 1968 classic horror film, *Night of the Living Dead*, takes nearly all the credit for inventing the modern zombie we know and love. Director George Romero transformed the major global fear of that era—the menacing threat of nuclear war between the United States and the Soviet Union—into a horror-packed bone chiller. Prior to Romero's film, only a few zombie movies had been made, and they mostly dramatized the Haitian myth. The villains of these movies were evil plantation owners who used black magic to create and exploit zombies.

George Romero changed everything—plot line, location, and characters. His setting was not a plantation but a single farmhouse where a small group of strangers fight the constant onslaught of zombies. The monsters hunt obsessively for fresh flesh to eat.

MASTER PUPPETEER

In 1818, Mary Wollstonecraft Shelley's Gothic novel *Frankenstein: or, The Modern Prometheus* popularized the dangers associated with the technological advances of the Industrial Revolution sweeping across England and Europe at the time.

Mary Wollstonecraft Shelley
(1797-1851)

The 2015 film *Victor Frankenstein* combines the powers of chemistry, **alchemy**, and electricity to reanimate a corpse patched together from body parts stolen from graveyards. Although Frankenstein's monster starts off as a childlike gentle giant, he eventually morphs into a murderous fiend. In many ways, the unintended consequences of creating the monster mirror those that people have long feared: a life dominated by machines, factories, and electronic gadgets.

Boris Karloff, who played Frankenstein's monster in the 1931 classic movie, is commemorated in this US stamp. *Frankenstein* shared some of the modern-day traits of zombies.

FAST FACT

In Greek mythology, a Titan named Prometheus stole fire from the gods and gave it to humankind. Fire has long been considered humanity's first great technological tool.

SCARY STORIES

A century after Mary Shelley spooked audiences with her science-inspired horror novel, the world suffered four years of unimaginable carnage: millions died on the battlefields of World War I. That slaughter was followed by the devastation of the Spanish influenza pandemic that wiped out even more people. Were Shelley's worries about science and technology an omen?

Not long after these tragedies, American writer H.P. Lovecraft began producing short stories about science run amok. His famous story, "The Call of Cthulhu," introduced readers to a nightmarish city of corpses—R'lyeh—perhaps the first zombies of popular fiction.

A REAL VICTOR FRANKENSTEIN

Scientist Luigi Galvani ran an electric current through dead bodies and made their muscles twitch. He called the phenomenon **galvanism**. In 1803, Galvani's nephew, Giovanni Aldini, used galvanism to scare the Royal College of Surgeons in London. He ran a steady current through a corpse, which caused the left eye to open, the fist to clench, and the mouth to quiver, as if it wanted to speak.

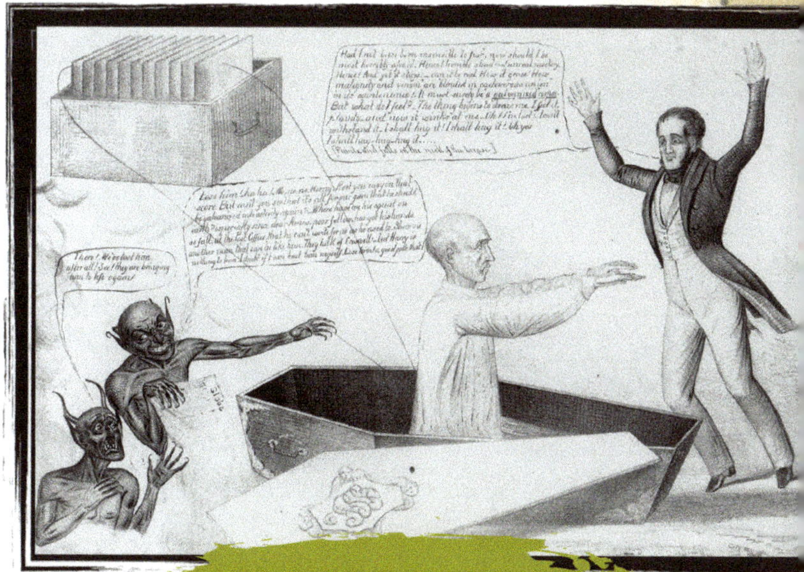

Electrical current appears to animate a corpse, shocking a spectator.

PULP FICTION

Many of today's top horror writers, such as Stephen King, mention Lovecraft as a major influence. However, Lovecraft never gained fame or fortune for his stories during his lifetime. The pulp magazines that published his stories, however, were extremely popular. By the 1950s, many of these comic books, including *Tales from the Crypt*, *Vault of Horror*, and *Weird Science* circulated a feast of stories featuring "man-made" zombies. As a boy, director George Romero enjoyed those stories, and they were a major influence on his development of the movie that would change the world's view of zombies.

If myths are the stories we tell again and again, it is no wonder that a few masterful storytellers quickly secured the zombie's place as the world's favorite monster.

In King's 2006 book, *Cell*, mobile phone signals turned humans into killer zombies.

FAST FACT

Stephen King was heavily influenced by H.P. Lovecraft.

A DEATH WISH

MASS HYSTERIAS AND DELUSIONS

In the menagerie of monsters, the zombie certainly emerges as a powerful symbol for war, pandemic illness, and death. Yet, how is it that so many eyewitnesses have claimed to see something that may never have existed? Have these accounts simply been cases of hysteria?

To be sure, history is full of mass hysterias. One famous example is the witch craze of the Middle Ages. It swept across the map for three centuries. Thousands claimed to have witnessed acts of witchcraft over the years. Another outbreak of mass hysteria was the Salem witch trials of colonial Massachusetts. In the brief span of a few months from 1692 to 1693, the wild stories resulted in 150 to 200 accusations of witchcraft, and 20 alleged witches were executed.

During the Salem witch trials, many so-called witches were tortured to confess, then convicted in courts and executed. This illustration of a witch trial is by Howard Pyle.

FOOD FOR THOUGHT

To better understand the historical eyewitness reports of vampires and werewolves, scientists probed the symptoms of many diseases. Applying the same methods to the zombie myth reveals a few surprising culprits.

The Fore people of Papua New Guinea traditionally practiced ritualistic cannibalism, eating the brains and vital organs of deceased elders. The practice was considered a show of deep respect and a means of passing on generational knowledge. Unfortunately, it also caused an outbreak of kuru, first discovered in the 1950s. Kuru is a progressive disease of the nervous system that causes pockets of air to form in the brain. Sufferers develop very zombie-like symptoms: jerking muscles, staggering gait, and delirious moaning.

Many people diagnosed with diseases of the nervous system—such as Alzheimer's and ALS (amyotrophic lateral sclerosis)—exhibit physical symptoms similar to those reported with kuru. In ancient times, observers who knew nothing about diseases of the brain might well have blamed such conditions on zombies.

In popular culture, zombies did not acquire a taste for brains until the 1985 film *Return of the Living Dead*.

FAST FACT

An infectious disease such as anthrax may have contributed to eyewitness testimonies of supposed zombies. The bacteria responsible for anthrax cause the skin to break out in black, oozing ulcers and sores—skin one might expect to see on a walking corpse.

DANGEROUS DRUG

Across parts of Russia and Eastern Europe today, the drug desomorphine is creating a different kind of walking dead. It is illegally sold on the streets as *krokodil* (crocodile), and users inject it.

Besides getting high, users develop patches of scaly, greenish-black crocodile skin, rancid open wounds, buckled bones and muscles, and scabby sores. Essentially, users rot from the inside out; however, they are too dazed to seek help.

BRAIN FOOD

In many countries, brains are considered a delicacy on the dinner table. In Pakistan and Bangladesh, *maghaz* is a mixture of fried animal brains topped with pistachios. *Gulai otak* is a kind of Indonesian curry made from cow brains.

"Bath salts" is a street drug originally sold disguised as minerals for bathing. As a white powder or crystals, the drug induces hallucinations and is very dangerous. In 2012 in Miami, Florida, an attacker high on "bath salts" chewed the face off one victim. He was dubbed the Miami Zombie.

THE KILLER INSIDE

Examining the scientific and biological roots of the zombie myth has also helped researchers observe "zombification" in nature. For example, the noble roly-poly, or pill bug, loves to eat bird poop. As if that weren't bad enough, the poop of some starlings can be infected with a parasite that takes over the roly-poly's brain. It forces the poor pill bug to dance around wildly out in the open where birds (maybe even a starling) will see it and eat it.

The pill bug has a segmented body. It can roll up into a ball to avoid being eaten by predators.

FAST FACT

The parasite in some starlings' poop is an acanthocephalan, also called the thorny-headed worm. "Akanthos" is Greek for thorny and "cephalon" means head.

MIND CONTROL

Like a voodoo *bokor*, wasps inject cockroaches with a powerful venom that paralyzes them in a death-like sleep. The roach can do nothing while its body turns into a container for wasp eggs. When the eggs hatch, the hungry larvae dine on the zombie roach.

A wasp paralyzes a cockroach with its venom.

Perhaps even more sinister is a fungus that takes hold of a carpenter ant's brain. No longer in control of itself, the ant wanders away from its colony and attaches itself to the underside of a leaf. Slowly, slowly—one nibble at a time—the fungus eats the ant alive from the inside! When all the food is gone, a stalk bursts out of the ant's head to spray more fungal spores into the air.

When a spore lands on a carpenter ant, a new victim is born.

HEADS UP

The real importance of zombies today lies not in what they can teach us about the past or the afterlife, but rather how we can live better right now and perhaps avoid a disastrous future.

In 2011, the US Centers for Disease Control and Prevention (CDC) sparked international interest in emergency response and preparation when they published a lighthearted blog post about how to survive a zombie apocalypse. The post went viral. Web traffic on the CDC's site swelled to 30,000 visits a day. Their Twitter followers jumped from 12,000 to 1.2 million!

There are now many sites on the Internet regarding a zombie apocalypse.

FAST FACT

On October 31, 2012, the US Marines, working with elite Navy personnel, staged a "zombie apocalypse" in order to test their capabilities in the event of a widespread human disaster.

SURVIVAL GUIDE

Later, the CDC and other emergency responders enacted "real" zombie apocalypses in order to test their response systems. Instead of imagining what might go wrong when society collapsed in the wake of a massive disaster, they pulled back the veil and watched.

As it turned out, successfully surviving a zombie apocalypse was just like surviving a massive natural disaster or terrorist attack. The survival strategies and tips appeared in the popular graphic novel, *Preparedness 101: Zombie Pandemic.*

FLUORIDE

During the Cold War, conspiracy theorists claimed that governments were adding fluoride to the public water supply in order to "zombify" entire countries. While some studies show that fluoride prevents tooth decay, the conspirators argued it weakened and poisoned the brain, making people more susceptible to control.

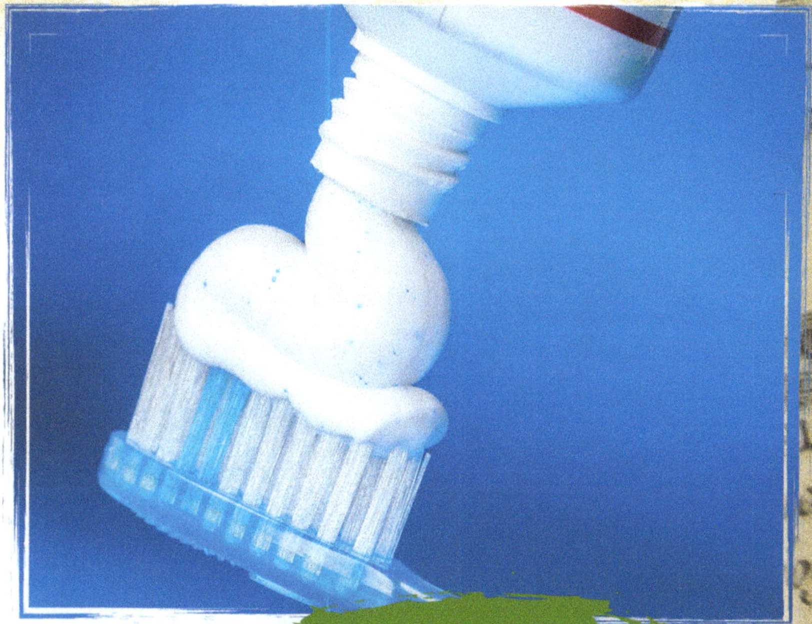

Some thought fluoride in toothpaste was used to control people.

LIVING CATASTROPHES

Given the proliferation of zombies throughout our global popular culture, we may seem to worship zombies like the *nzambi* gods from which they stem. Over time, the zombie myth has grown larger than its roots. It has truly taken over our inner spirit. According to *voudon* traditions, spiritual possession can be a good thing. It is an opportunity to be in closer contact with greater powers in the universe.

For these reasons, it might be wise for humans to keep telling zombie myths. After all, we are genetically designed to die. If we cannot escape our fate, at least we can let the zombie be our guide.

Zombification could spread through the world like a fast epidemic.

ZOMBIE MYTHS ACROSS THE MAP

Here are some of the places where zombie myths originated.

MAP KEY

1. Alberta
2. Bangladesh
3. Brazil
4. Canada
5. Caribbean Sea
6. Central America
7. China
8. Democratic Republic of the Congo
9. Denmark
10. England
11. Germany
12. Greece
13. Haiti
14. Hollywood
15. Iceland
16. India
17. Indonesia
18. Iraq
19. Ireland
20. Israel
21. Italy
22. Japan
23. Louisiana
24. Massachusetts
25. Mexico
26. Missouri
27. Montana
28. North Dakota
29. Norway
30. Pakistan
31. Papua New Guinea
32. Pennsylvania
33. Portugal
34. Russia
35. Saudi Arabia
36. Sweden
37. Syria
38. Texas
39. Ukraine
40. Venezuela

GLOSSARY

alchemy a medieval chemical science that sought to convert metals into gold and discover universal cures for diseases and elixirs for immortality

autolysis a process by which cells are digested by enzymes or bacteria

catatonic in an unresponsive state

corroborate to support with evidence

decapitate to cut off a head

exhume to dig something out of the ground

extinction the end of a species

galvanism the contraction of muscles using electrical currents

neurotoxin a poisonous substance that acts on the nervous system

pandemic a disease outbreak that spreads across one or more continents

revenant a person who returns from death

rigor mortis temporary stiffness of muscles occurring after death

terracotta a reddish-brown baked clay used for pottery, statues, and building materials

FURTHER INFORMATION

BOOKS

Brallier, Max. *The Last Kids on Earth*. New York: Viking, 2015.

Maberry, John. *Rot & Ruin* (series). New York: Simon & Schuster, 2010–2015.

Montandon, Max. *The Proper Care and Feeding of Zombies: A Completely Scientific Guide to the Lives of the Undead*. New York: Wiley, 2010.

Tobin, Paul and Chan, Ron. *Plants vs Zombies* (series). Toronto: Dark Horse Books, 2013–2017.

Vuckovic, Jovanka and Romero, George A. *Zombies!: An Illustrated History of the Undead*. New York: St. Martin's Griffin, 2011.

WEBSITES

Learn more about Día de los Muertos here!
latino.si.edu/dayofthedead/

Prepare for the zombie apocalypse with these tips from the Centers for Disease Control and Prevention!
blogs.cdc.gov/publichealthmatters/2011/05/preparedness-101-zombie-apocalypse/

INDEX

bath salts (drug), 39
Booth, Douglas, 32
Burton, Tim, 17, 32
"Call of Cthulhu, The" (story) 35
Cell (novel), 36
Corpse Bride (film), 17
Dahmer, Jeffrey, 24
Davis, Wade, 11, 12
Día de Muertos, 20
diseases, 5, 13, 19, 22, 25, 26, 27, 38, 42, 44
Dungeons & Dragons (game), 32
Frankenstein: or, The Modern Prometheus (novel), 34
fugu fish, 12
Galvani, Luigi, 35
Gilgamesh, Epic of, 16
Huangdi, Qin Shi, 27
Hurston, Zora Neale, 10
Karloff, Boris, 34
King, Stephen, 36
Kuru, 38
Laveau, Marie, 8
Lord of the Rings (novels), 32
Lovecraft, H.P., 35, 36
ma'nene, 20
Marion, Isaac, 31
Martin, George R.R., 32
Miss Peregrine's Home for Peculiar Children (novel & film), 32
Night of the Living Dead (film), 33
pandemic, 5, 22, 35, 37, 43
Pride and Prejudice and Zombies (novel & film), 32
Pyle, Howard, 37
Resident Evil (films), 31
Return of the Living Dead (film), 38
revenant, 14
Riggs, Ransom, 32
Romero, George, 33, 36
Shelley, Mary Wollstonecraft, 34, 35
Song of Ice and Fire, A (novel series), 32
Swift Runner, 19, 24
Tales from the Crypt (comic), 36
Terracotta Army, 27
Tolkien, J.R.R., 32
toxins, 10, 11, 12
Vault of Horror (comic), 36
voodoo, 7, 8, 9, 10, 11, 12, 19, 28, 41
Walking Dead, The (film), 31
Warm Bodies (film), 31
witches, 18, 37
World of Warcraft (game), 32
zombie walks, 30